Fuzzy Red Bathrobe

Questions from the Heart for Mothers & Daughters

by

Carol Lynn Pearson & Emily Pearson

with illustrations by

Traci O'Very Covey

Salt Lake City

For Katy—with all our love.

First Edition
05 04 03 02 01 00   5 4 3 2 1

Published by
Gibbs Smith, Publisher
P.O. Box 667
Layton, Utah 84041

Toll-free orders: (1-800) 748-5439
Web site: www.gibbs-smith.com

Edited by Suzanne Taylor
Designed and produced by Traci O'Very Covey
Printed in Hong Kong

Library of Congress Cataloging-in-Publication Data
Pearson, Carol Lynn.
  Fuzzy red bathrobe: questions from the heart for mothers and
daughters / by Carol Lynn Pearson and Emily Pearson; illustrated by
Traci O'Very Covey.—1st ed.
    p. cm.
  ISBN 1-58685-003-2
  1. Mothers and daughters—United States. 2. Communication in
the family—United States. I. Pearson, Emily. II. Title.
HQ755.85 .P39 2000
306.874'3—dc21   00-023761

CONTENTS

LIKE MY MOTHER

Emily

I WISH THAT I COULD SING THIS introduction. Or better yet, I wish it was a monologue, written by someone *else*, and I was on stage ready to perform it. I am sitting here at my computer staring at my mother's introduction, paralyzed by the taunting in my head, "Go ahead, compete with *this!*"

When I was a little girl people always asked me if I was going to grow up to be a writer like my mother. "No!" I would emphatically answer, "I am going to be an actress." "Oh, an actress—like your mother."

Like my mother.

Why have I spent so much energy trying to be anything but "like my mother"

I look around me in this garden behind my mother's house. It has become a wave of light, an affirmation that rises not only beyond sorrow, but from a sense of wondering joy. I glance quickly at my mother, who has fallen silent, and I watch with disbelief the way the distance between us, and all separation, heals over.

—KIM CHERNIN

In My Mother's House

when so much of who I am is so interwoven with who she is? She is one of the most amazing people I have ever known.

♥ ♥ ♥

FOR AS LONG AS I CAN REMEMBER there was this enormous thing keeping me from having a close relationship with my mom—my dad. To me, my dad was the sun, the moon, and the stars. He was Disneyland, Christmas, and a never-ending birthday party. When they were divorced, he got to be Peter Pan, and she got to be structure, rules, and, well, not a lot of the fun stuff. I was never actually told that I had to choose between my parents, but it was very clear to my ten-year-old brain that in order to maintain my place as his princess, I had to choose him in everything. And I did. I chose him. I chose the party.

I was about twelve the first time I vocally acknowledged to a friend that my dad was gay. I had never spoken with anyone about it, but it was something I had somehow always known. After I told my mom that I knew, my dad officially "came out" to me. He was so relieved by my continued unconditional love for him and so excited to share his world with me that suddenly it was as if I was no longer his young daughter. I was a mini grown-up, a little him, spending weekends with him at his apartment on Castro Street in San Francisco, going to the Gay Day festivals and parades. Unbeknownst to my mother and against her wishes, I wandered wide-eyed through gay bookstores and bars and streets filled with beautiful, well-built men hugging and kissing each other. Drag queens became my dearest friends. I was always safe and loved and adored—and

invisible. It didn't take long to notice that the men only looked at each other, all wanted each other. Unless my father specifically drew attention to me, or unless I was dressed up like Marilyn Monroe, it was like I wasn't even there. I was a female in a world of men who didn't want females. I was loved and accepted because I was a little girl, but if I had been a woman I feared I would have been rejected—like my mother. I developed a fear of growing up and becoming an unlovable woman. If my mom, with her brilliance and wit and beautiful eyes, wasn't good enough, how could I ever be? I would just have to be different. I would have to be totally different from my mom. But how? How does a girl become a woman while at the same time rejecting her mother and her own femininity? She doesn't.

♥ ♥ ♥

MY DAD PASSED AWAY DUE TO complications from AIDS when I was sixteen. I was left feeling so totally alone and empty. I had no idea about who

I was. I knew who my dad was, and what he thought, and what he felt, but I had lost myself. My dad was gone, but my mom was there. She had always been there, paying the bills, driving us to school, and fixing our dinner. Now she was there to let me sleep in her bed every night and to hold me while I cried. Sometimes she did a great job of comforting and saying just the right thing, and sometimes she didn't. But she was always there doing the very best she could. Just being there was a remarkable thing.

Several years of depression followed. Not even knowing how to look for myself, I looked to men to tell me who I was and to answer all my questions. I looked to men to love and to validate me. I was looking for my father. Needless to say, I made some *really* bad dating choices. And mom was always there. She was the voice on the other end of the phone telling me that she loved me and to hang on, and she was there to hold interventions with me and my boyfriends when it was clear to both of us

that I needed extra help and support. I felt weak, needy, and very lost. However, deep down in the very most inner part of my soul was the knowledge and vision of the woman I really was, or the woman I desperately wanted to become. I could see her clearly in my mind, yet I had no idea how to get from where I was to where she was.

One summer I was at Lake Powell in southern Utah, one of my favorite places on earth, and I noticed a little sunflower that had sprouted underneath a section of red-rock cliff. Remarkably it had pushed its way through the rock toward the sunshine and was now growing strong and straight right in the middle of the cliff. I stared at that little superhero flower for a very long time. It reminded me that I had been pushing with all my strength against my own rock for so many years. This sunflower was like a divine promise that I would feel the sun again someday.

After a decade of the right therapists, books, friends, songs, movies, and prayers, my roots and stem have been healed, and I am stretching toward the sun. The inward healing journey has been more painful and more joyous than I could ever have imagined, and I wouldn't trade one moment of it for anything. Yes, there has been much rain in my garden, but, as my mother so aptly puts it, this little flower grew where she was planted in spite of it all.

♥ ♥ ♥

I HAVE BEEN MARRIED FOR NEARLY SIX years and have two children. My four-year-old Christian and two-year-old Tara have been instrumental in assisting me in my never-ending quest for womanhood. Feeling life growing inside of me left little doubt in my mind that I was—am—in fact, a woman. While seven months pregnant with Christian, I watched the video *A Child Is Born,* in which the conception and growth of an embryo is filmed in full color. I was awestruck to see the sperm meet the egg and then to literally fill it with generations of genetic information. I realized that my child was being made up of Steven's parents and their parents and their parents

and my parents and their parents and their parents. I sat there on the couch feeling ancient blood course through my veins. Not only am I made up of countless combinations of hair color, eye color, height, and mannerisms, but, with all that is known about cell memory, perhaps I also have the hopes and dreams, likes and dislikes, joy and pain of a hundred grandfathers and grandmothers. Why have I loved dolls all of my life? Maybe it is because my great-grandmother Sarah collected dolls and had to leave every one of them behind in England to come to a new country and walk across the plains. Maybe I heard that story enough times as a child to be influenced by it, or perhaps there is some deep remembering in my body and soul.

Whether it is stories or cells or both, the men—and especially the women—who came before me paved the way for me to be who I am now. Did I inherit my love of theater from not only my parents but also my grandmother Emeline, whose copies of *King Lear* and *Twelfth Night* I own? I detest extreme heat as did my great-great-grand-mother Mary, who refused to settle in Mesa, Arizona, with her husband and spent the rest of her life in Dingle Dell, Idaho. I know I absolutely did *not* inherit my great-great-grandmother Esther Ann's ability to give birth to my fourteenth child under a covered wagon in the worst snowstorm in history, covered with lice! (I will be eternally grateful for hospitals and epidurals.) But I do feel a closeness to her. Is she my guardian angel? Maybe they all are. Perhaps they have all been by my side watching over me, weeping with me, cheering for me, and inspiring me. All these years have they been actively assisting in my healing and then, in turn, being healed themselves? The only thing I really know is that fifteen years after the death of my father, I have made a most miraculous journey into womanhood, and I know that I have not done it alone. I had my friends, my family, my husband, my children, my therapists, my angels, and my mother.

♥   ♥   ♥

I HAVE READ COUNTLESS ARTICLES stating that depression is repressed anger. I was intensely angry after losing my dad: angry that he was gone, angry that I was alone, angry that my mom tried to fix it all and make it all okay and that she couldn't, angry that my siblings and I seemed unable to connect or love each other like before, angry that no one in my family seemed able to give me what I needed. Everything blew apart and was never quite the same. No matter how I tried, I seemed unable to arrive at a place of peace with my mother, brothers, or my sister. My Katy.

When I was seven years old I got the little sister that I had been longing for. Katy was more like my own child than my sister. When we were young, the bond we had was so strong that we used to say that we would marry Siamese twins so that we could always be together. After our dad died, I was plunged into a darkness that took me far away from Katy. We still loved each other, but there was so much baggage between and all around us that we had a hard time connecting and reaching each other.

Years passed. I got married, had children, and moved to Connecticut; she grew up and got married. I always figured that one day we would find one another again. Nine months ago I received the phone call telling me that my little sister had experienced a massive seizure, a large brain tumor had been found, and she was in a coma with only a few days to live. Everything began to spin. I packed up my kids, caught a plane in time to get there to say good-bye, and watched her fly away. I felt numb and barely able to function. Everyone, including myself, expected me to fall to pieces. I didn't. I was going to sing the song at her funeral that had always brought me to tears thinking of Katy, and I thought I wouldn't make it through. I did. And as I was standing at the microphone singing to her, I closed my eyes and something amazing happened. I can't explain how it happened, but in those few

minutes, my issues with my family vanished, and I became acutely aware of two new things I had become: my mother's only daughter and, finally, a woman.

In the months that followed I was grieving deeply but still aware that things were shifting and growing and changing inside of me. One night my mom and I were in her hot tub and she began weeping. I held her in my arms and found myself rocking her and singing her the lullabies that she had written for Katy and me and had sung to us when we were children. As I was holding my mother, I felt Katy and my grandmother Emeline there with us, very involved in what was going on. My mom and I were moving into a brand-new place in our relationship, and I was moving into a brand-new place inside myself. I felt a little afraid, very incapable, and totally thrilled.

♥ ♥ ♥

WHEN MY MOM AND I FIRST BEGAN working on this book, I felt a bit uncomfortable getting into any deep sharing. I wondered why that was. Was it left over from my rejection of her and of myself as a woman? Was I just not used to trusting myself to stand on my own two feet as a grown-up woman, or afraid of seeing too much of myself in her or of her in me? In the end I decided that it really didn't matter why, and I didn't need to continue analyzing it, I just needed to get over it. I dove in and had such a great time. We giggled about first kisses and old jokes and learned more about each other's dreams. I couldn't get over the fact that, as a child, my mom had begged her parents for an accordion. An accordion! When she stated that the one thing she would do differently would be to make herself beautiful every morning and put on perfume so that we would associate her with that more than with her fuzzy red bath-

robe, I was touched and have made an effort to do the same. And after learning the history behind that bathrobe, I see it as a comforting hug my mom wears, and I never want her to get rid of it.

I have always known my mom pretty well, but now I know "us" a lot better. Who she is has greatly influenced who I am, and who I am has greatly influenced who she is. In many ways we are vastly different and complement each other. And in other ways, we are very much alike, and that's okay. It's better than okay—it's wonderful. I have inherited her strength, her wit, her ability to have great lifelong friendships, and my daughter has her dimple.

I am a performer, a wife, a mother, a daughter, a friend, a sister, yes—a writer—and a woman.

Just like my mother.

AN OLDER EQUAL

Carol Lynn

EMILY WAS COMING HOME FOR A month with her two children. Mothering and grandmothering for a solid month sounded intimidating. And delightful. Em and her husband were moving from the East Coast to the West, and she was burned out with being a grad-school wife in a cramped apartment. A month of being mothered sounded irresistible.

The timing was poignant. Only three months before, Emily and her two brothers and I had stood around the bed of her younger sister, Katy, as she took her flight from this world to the next, only a short while after having been diagnosed with a rapidly growing brain tumor. At the bedside and then the funeral, Emily had broken the hearts of everyone present by singing "Wind Beneath My Wings." Later, she had held me while I howled.

Dear Emily. Dear always for her warmth, her razor wit, her huge and vulnerable heart, her wonderful voice and theatrical talent. Dear for being the first child, the first daughter— and now the only daughter. It's not that mothers love their daughters more than they love their sons. It's just that, besides the love, there is the shared journey on

The simple act of consciously creating a space to hear your mother's or grandmother's story, from her point of view, can have a transformative effect on your relationship. Many women go through life without ever being asked how it was for them, what the meaning of their life experience has been. When you ask for your mother's story you are making her the heroine of the drama. You may be surprised at how moved she is, and how willing to share her life experience . . . . The central question to ask is: "What was it like for you?"
—NAOMI RUTH LOWINSKY
Stories from the Motherline

that wonderful ride of femaleness, for which only those two X chromosomes give you a ticket.

So Emily was coming! For a month! How many such protected times would we have before she sang at my deathbed, or I at hers? What if, by some strange fortune, this visit would be our last?

I had to make this month count. I would drop my life and try to be the mother she had always deserved: baking those apple pies that made her swoon, massaging her feet with lavender oil, getting up early with the children so she could sleep, brushing her hair, sitting together in the hot tub under the stars, making sure she knew all my good stories, what I'd been learning lately, what I'd been reading, thinking, making sure I knew how she had really been experiencing Katy's passing, her own wifehood, motherhood, that tofu recipe I had dictated over the phone.

Yes. If I had a month with Emily, and if it were my last month, I'd want to make sure she really knew me, and that I really

knew her. What rooms in the house of my soul had she not been invited into? What rooms in her house did I think I knew but in truth had never noticed or never knocked on? What precious furnishings were lying about unappreciated, what hidden dreams, trivial incidents, or funny and embarrassing stories? We were now two adult women, one almost sixty, one half that. And what did Emily not know of the life and soul of my mother, Emeline, after whom she was named, who had died long before she was born but who had given her genes and had molded her mother? I began to make notes about things I wanted to tell my daughter, to ask her. Exciting. Scary.

That's how this book was born.

♥ ♥ ♥

WE MET, EMILY AND I, WHEN I was twenty-nine and two years married. When her father and I had decided it was time for a child, we sent out the invitation every day for a month. Invitation received and confirmed. From my diary:

"Tuesday, November 28, 1967. It's

true. I'm going to be a mother. Right now there is a little being inside of me, growing and becoming a person. I feel happy about it, calm. . . . Gerald, of course, is delighted. In fact, if my visit today had revealed that I wasn't pregnant, I wouldn't have dared come home until I was!"

On June 21, 1968, she arrived. The diary again: "About three-thirty the next morning I woke up with some contractions. . . . I didn't want to turn on the light to time them, so I recited poetry to myself. It takes me exactly one minute to recite a sonnet, so I went through some of Elizabeth Barrett Browning. I discovered that the contractions were about three minutes apart. . . . So I figured something serious was going on."

After the delivery, done naturally and without complications, after the delicious hour under the warm blanket in the recovery room, I got up for the first time to go to the bathroom. There, in the mirror, something unusual, something different about my eyes. Something very subtle, but

something to do with light. A tiny shaft of triumph, perhaps, or a glint of possibility.

A few pages later in the diary I wrote a poem:

MOTHER TO CHILD
Look—
Your little fist fits mine
Like the pit in a plum.
I think,
In the time before remembering,
These two hands
Clasped companionably,
Then parted.
Help me, child.
Forgive me when I fail you.
I'm your mother, true,
But in the end
Merely an older equal
Doing her faltering best
For a dear, small
Friend.

♥ ♥ ♥

MY FALTERING BEST. GIVING TO Emily all that was in my knapsack, unable to give her what was not there, just as I knew Emeline had given me everything in her own knapsack. I had carried my daughter for nine months, but I carried other women for much longer. Just as Maxine Kumin had written:

Like those old pear-shaped Russian dolls that open at the middle to reveal another and another, down to the peasized, irreducible minimum . . . we carry our mothers forth in our bellies.

Back to the beginning. Shared genes, cells, memories, limitations. I, Carol Lynn, was born of Emeline who taught school and died when I was fifteen, who was born of Sarah who left her dolls in Nottingham and walked across the plains beside a covered wagon when she was eight, who was born of Mary the wife of the lacemaker who left it all to follow truth across the sea.

That's as far as the stories take me. Those are the dolls I can feel cupped inside my spiritual belly. My motherline. We poured into Emily our lives along with the rich milk that flowed so effortlessly from my breasts.

♥ ♥ ♥

A FEW WEEKS AGO I CALLED EMILY and said, "Montel Williams is having a show called 'Daughters Who Are Desperate for Their Mother's Attention.' I thought if you are going to be on it, I would try to watch. On the other hand, I'm really busy." She laughed.

This morning I called and left a message on her machine. "Emily. Montel Williams is having a show called 'Young Women Who Feel Their Mothers Have Ruined Their Lives.' If you are going to be on it, let me know, and I promise to watch." I giggled and hung up.

Ruined their lives? Can mothers ruin their lives? Yes, mothers can be abusive, cruel, inattentive. But what if it's true, this proposition I've come to accept—that we magnetize into our lives precisely the people and the events that are necessary for our next steps in growing? What if it's true that life, God, the universe conspire to plant us each in the right garden?

On my refrigerator there are five

charming flower-basket magnets that Emily gave me last year, each featuring a word: "Grow—Where—You—Are—Planted." She'd heard me say that often. What if that is more than just a wise saying?

What if each of us has been planted perfectly? My mother, Emeline, was not perfect, but what if she was perfect for me? Carol Lynn is not perfect, but what if she is perfect for Emily? What if my mother's garden gave me the sun that I needed and the rain that I needed? And Emily's the same? What if life, God, the universe, are constantly kind and we do have all of eternity?

♥ ♥ ♥

TWO-YEAR-OLD TARA NEVER KNEW it during that month at Grandma Blossom's house, but her great-grandmother Emeline was present in so many of the moments we shared—in the lullaby I sang her. "Baby's boat's a silver moon, sailing in the sky"—in the poem I said as I pushed her swing at the park—"How do you like to go up in the swing, up in the air so blue?"—in the little tap dance I did on the bathroom floor as I entertained her and Christian while they were in the bathtub—step-shuffle-shuffle-step, "East side, west side, all around the town."

♥ ♥ ♥

EMELINE CRIED A LOT. THAT WAS the rain. When Emily asked the question "What is one of the first memories you have of your mother?" my response came easily.

Her crying.

It wasn't just the work of bearing and raising five children, beginning at age thirty-nine with twins; it wasn't just being moved from the city to the Indian reservation where we used kerosene lamps and heated water that we pumped from a well even when it was forty degrees below. It had something to do with disappointing herself in some way about what a mother was supposed to be. I think of my mother's breast cancer now when I read yet again of that disease specializing in women who have the "martyr syndrome," whose breasts and hearts give and give and do not express and claim their own needs.

When I asked Emily the same question, "What is a first memory you have of your mother?" I held my breath.

She was quiet for a moment. Then, "Oh, you standing at the stove and belting out songs with Judy Garland."

Whew!

And plenty of memories of my sadness too, my stoic resolve, my tight-lipped determination to get from one day to the next. But flowing in and out of the sad memories, there I was, belting out songs with Judy Garland.

"Tell me a joke your mother has told you," I said to Emily in one of our quiz adventures.

"Oh, right!" she said. "How about twenty-nine million of them?"

That's one thing I will take credit for. I remember, adapt, and make up jokes. There's a whole section in my day planner devoted to jokes.

"Well, Mom, I bet you can't tell me a joke your mother told you."

"Wrong. An aristocratic Irish potato married a sweet potato and they had a baby potato. The Irish potato asked the baby potato what she wanted to do when she grew up. The baby potato said, 'I want to marry Edward R. Murrow.' 'What?' said the Irish potato. 'Why, you can't marry Edward R. Murrow. He's just a common-tater!'"

A spot of sun.

Oh, a great deal of sun. The lullaby, the poems, the step-shuffle-shuffle-step, the admonition to have lots of friends, not just one, the encouraging letters she wrote to each of us and put in our stockings on her last Christmas, the handkerchief that I had cried into, cleaned and pressed, and given to me with the words, "You've had it in happy times and in sad, there'll be more of both. Keep it and remember."

Her rain a blessing too. Easiest is not always best. I am deeper, richer because of my mother's rain. I have had to reach further, within and without. Even her leaving awoke in me hungers, awarenesses, and sensitivities that have served me.

♥ ♥ ♥

BUT MY EMILY'S GARDEN WAS GOING to be sunny! No storms for this precious seed.

I could not have predicted the huge storm.

Well, perhaps I could have, but I was so naive, so hopeful, so determined.

Emily's father, Gerald, was a beautiful man—blond, charming, filled with light. He was also a man who struggled with a homosexual orientation. Even knowing this, I wanted him. And he loved me, to the very best of his ability.

So many sunny days.

Emily's friends envied her father—so fun, so warm, so in love with his children. He cooked elegant meals for the family. He borrowed money and published my first book. He showed off his brilliant two-year-old at every opportunity. "Emily, what did Romeo say to Juliet?"

The reply came confidently and with an endearing lisp: "Goodnight, goodnight, parting is such sweet sorrow that I shall say goodnight 'til it be morrow."

The rain clouds were gathering very early, but the storm did not break until Emily was eight and the three other dear ones had arrived. And then the torrent, the anguish, several years of agony. When we told the children, Emily cried. She was the oldest and recognized the word divorce.

Oh, this was not what I had in mind for my Emily, for the others. Not the end of a marriage, not the six years of confusion that followed, knowing her father loved her dearly but could not really be a father to her, seeing him give himself to a lifestyle that was frightening, even brutal. Oh, certainly not sitting again with the family for more news, this time that her father was suffering with AIDS.

Never, never was there a thought that this sweet baby drinking life from my breast would be saying, "Good-bye, good-bye, I love you," to her father as he took his last breaths, lying on the couch in the family home where he was being cared for through his death.

♥ ♥ ♥

RAIN IN EMILY'S GARDEN? OH, I think so.

Smooth sailing between the daughter and the mother? I think not.

I did not recognize that Emily needed more help than she received to deal with the divorce and then the death. Pioneer-like, I got behind the wagon every morning and gritted my teeth and put one foot in front of the other. That's how we do things. That's how even the children have to do things.

Later, sitting with Emily in a therapist's office, I cried. I didn't know her pain was so great. I didn't know of other hurts that had found their way into her life, hurts I seemed to have no tools for preventing or for acknowledging or soothing.

There must be a time or two in every mother's journey when she feels she has failed so hugely that it's time to say the

closing prayer, give a bitter benediction on this awful thing we call life, and just curl up and wait for it to be over.

But we don't. We get up each morning and we put on our fuzzy red bathrobe and we do the best we can to warm ourselves and the ones we love. And as we dare to trust them, they come to understand and we are grateful to know that they understand. And we each forgive. I really believe that when we understand, it becomes easy to forgive. In one of our question-and-answer sessions, I said, "Well, Emily, speaking of the fuzzy red bathrobe that I've worn for what seems like forever, do you know the story behind it?"

"No. What is it?" she replied.

"I got it during that terrible autumn when my life fell apart, when I knew my marriage was not what I had thought it was. I was numb, in such pain, and always cold, inside and out. One day downtown in one of the upscale stores I was riding the escalator and I looked up to see on display a beautiful, plush, crimson bathrobe. Oh, I wanted it! It had been so long since I had felt beautiful or comforted, or even really warm. But it was fifty dollars. I never spent that kind of money on something for myself. I went back to the store once, twice, until finally I bought it. And it gave me comfort and warmth. I know it's become a family joke, but in the beginning it was a blessing to me, a statement from myself that I was worth spending fifty dollars on."

♥ ♥ ♥

RUIN THEIR LIVES?

The rain stops. The sun comes out. The little flower grows where she was planted in spite of it all.

Watching Emily grow. Oh, my. Montel should do a show called "Mothers Who Are Awestruck to Watch Their Daughters Grow." I watch Emily unfold, watch like I would watch a play that I've never seen before, one that I can tell has been written by a sure hand and is being performed by an artist. Her humor cracks me up. Her patience with her children amazes me. Her developing insights into life thrill me. "You

know what?" she said last week on the telephone. "All my life I've been looking outside myself for the answers. I'm not going to do that anymore. I know the answers are all inside of me. That's where I'm going to look."

♥ ♥ ♥

THE OTHER DAY I GOT A POSTCARD Emily had sent me from a zoo they had visited. On the front are two giraffes, foreheads pressed together, one with a longer neck stretching down to touch the one with the smaller face. "Mom—this picture reminded me of you and me . . . I love you! Em."

The smaller giraffe is Emily. I guess. That's the child. The taller giraffe is me. I guess. I'm the mother.

. . . But in the end,
Merely an older equal
Doing her faltering best
For a dear, small
Friend.

♥ ♥ ♥

Suggestions for Using This Book

1. Take turns answering the questions according to what each believes the other thinks or has experienced. The other then responds, sharing how she really feels.

2. Write in it if you feel like it. Don't if you don't feel like it.

3. If you find the conversations take you into unexpectedly troubled waters, find a competent professional to guide you through them. This experience is not meant to take the place of needed therapy.

4. Drop any section that doesn't interest you. Create new sections. Change the questions; add new ones.

5. The questions are phrased as if the daughter is now grown. If she does not have experience in the question asked, adapt it to what she might feel in the future or what she is feeling now.

6. You don't have to be in the same room. A long-distance session on Sunday at five cents a minute can be wonderful.

7. When "Grandmother" is mentioned, it suggests the mother's mother. Try to invite her experience and point of view, then the other grandmother, even mothers before them.

8. Listen. Learn. Love.

Ancestors and Family

In what situations do I ever think about an ancestor?

What ancestor do I admire for something in particular?

What kind of relationship did I have with my grandmothers? With my grandfathers?

The mother!
She is what keeps
the family intact…
It is proved.
—ANNA F. TREVISAN

Do I own an artifact or history that belonged to a female ancestor? Do I display it or have I read it?

There is probably
nothing like living
together for
blinding people to
each other.
—IVY COMPTON-
BURNETT

What physical characteristics do I feel I have inherited from my mother and grandmothers?

A family unity
which is only bound
together with a
table-cloth is of
questionable value.
—CHARLOTTE
PERKINS GILMAN

What positive qualities do I feel or hope I have inherited from my mother and grand-mothers?

Is there a time I came to understand my own mother more? How did that time help me see her better? Do I feel a need to understand her better now?

Name my siblings in chronological order. Which of them do I feel that I am most like? Most unlike? How has my relationship with them changed over the years?

Some ancestor . . . who fought with the Ironsides, or protested with the Covenanters, or legislated with the Puritans, may, at this very hour, be influencing us, in a way of which we never speak, and in which no other soul intermeddles.

—AMELIA BARR

Did either of my parents or grandparents have a pet name for me when I was little?

Do I feel I was placed in my particular family for a reason? Have I figured it out yet?

Do I feel that my birth order in the family has affected my life?

When one person in a family (the patient) has pain which shows up in symptoms, all family members are feeling this pain in some way.

—VIRGINIA SATIR

What is my full maiden name? Where was I born? When was I born? Was there anything unusual about my birth?

What is Grandmother's full maiden name? Where was she born? When was she born?

Where did she grow up? Where did she meet her husband?

What is an interesting story about her life?

What is a strength she had?

What decision did she make that affected us both?

What is one dream she fulfilled? What is one dream she never fulfilled?

Can you answer any of the above questions regarding Grandmother's mother?

Each say out loud using first names:
"I am _____, the daughter of
_____, who is the
daughter of _____,
who is the daughter of _____."
(Go back as far as you can go.)

What can a grand-mother offer . . . ? Of course. My own small footnote. The homemade bread at the banquet. The private joke in the divine comedy. Your roots. This, then, is the grandmother's special gift—a bridge to your past.
—HELEN HAYES

When we step up to the mirror it's usually our mother, not our grandmother, whom we're afraid to see.
—HOPE EDELMAN

Bodies and Health

Which one of your physical characteristics have I always thought was beautiful?

How did I feel about my body when I was little? In adolescence? Now?

What hairstyle do I like most on you?

As I look around the West End these days, it seems to me that outside every thin girl is a fat man, trying to get in.

—KATHARINE WHITEHORN

Do I shave my legs? How far up? Armpits? The hair on my toes? Do I have polish on my toenails right now?

If I know I'm going to be in the house all day, do I still do a full makeup? How do I dress?

But what was a body? Dust, dung, urine, itches. It was the light within which was important.

—TAYLOR CALDWELL

What do I think about cosmetic surgery? Do I know someone who has had it? Have I ever wanted it for myself?

If I had to do without one of my senses, which one would I *not* give up?

Are there foods I eat that I don't especially like but eat for health reasons?

What is the greatest physical pain I have ever experienced? Broken bones? Surgeries?

Do I have any allergies? What is my blood type?

What health problems have I overcome? What health problems am I working on now? What health problems have I learned to live with?

I think what is happening to me is so wonderful, and not only what can be seen on my body, but all that is taking place inside.

—ANNE FRANK

How many hours of sleep do I think I need? How many do I usually get? Do I snore? Grind my teeth?

Cell by cell, you replace yourself. Thought by thought, you create yourself. Dream by dream, you envision the universe.

—SUSUN S. WEED

How much water do I drink during the day? Do I feel that is enough?

Do I feel I am a friend to my body? What do I do for it? What do I feel I should be doing for my body that I'm not now doing?

What is my favorite form of exercise?
Least favorite?

How do I feel about holistic and traditional approaches to healing? Chiropractic? Acupuncture? Massage? Other unconventional approaches?

Do I feel I handle stress well? If not, how does it affect my body and how do I feel I could handle it better?

Have I ever been clinically depressed? How was that handled?

Do I expect to live past ninety?

How do I believe Grandmother felt about her body? What was her experience with her health?

Heal *comes from the same root as* whole *and* holiness.
—BROOKE
MEDICINE EAGLE

I believe most people need to learn to love themselves again in order to truly heal themselves.
—LOUISE HAY

Being a Woman

What do I love about being a woman?

What do I hate about being a woman?

Have I ever wanted to be a man?

Do I feel my parents were happy that I was born a girl?

What attitudes about femaleness did I absorb from my mother?

What attitudes about femaleness did I absorb from my father?

Do I feel women are innately different from men? How?

How did I experience my transition from girl-hood to womanhood? What do I feel I gained? What do I feel I lost?

What did I feel about beginning menstruation?

The art of being a woman can never consist of being a bad imitation of a man.

—OLGA KNOPF

To a disturbing degree, we don't want to be like our mothers. Why should we want to be like them, we might ask, since so much of what they do is ignored or devalued? Isn't that like wanting to be a welfare recipient or a kid in the slow reading group?

—PAULA J. CAPLAN

What sort of menstrual periods have I had?
What is my experience with PMS?

How did I feel about getting my first bra?

How have I felt in the past and how do I feel
now about the size of my breasts?

Men are taught to apologize for their weaknesses, women for their strengths.

—LOIS WYSE

What kind of sex education did I receive, and
do I feel it was adequate?

We still think of a powerful man as a born leader and a powerful woman as an anomaly.

—MARGARET ATWOOD

Do I, have I, or do I believe I could, enjoy
sex?

What do I think of the "woman's movement"?
In what ways do I or do I not consider myself
a feminist?

What do I think about mothers working
outside the home?

What do I think about abortion?

Would I like to see a woman as U.S. president?

Who do I feel has been a good female role model for me?

What do I think Grandmother felt about being a woman?

A liberated woman is one who feels confident in herself, and is happy in what she is doing. She is a person who has a sense of self.
—BETTY FORD

What seems to happen to girls is this: They start full of enthusiasm, ready to climb. . . . Somewhere along the trip up the ladder to adulthood, girls get their fingers stepped on and they quit climbing.
—JUDY MANN

Birth and Child-Rearing

How did I feel when I first learned I was pregnant?

What kind of pregnancies did I have, physically and emotionally?

How many hours was I in labor with each of my children? What medications were used? Were there any complications? Who was present at each birth? How did I feel about my doctor or midwife?

In the final analysis it is not what you do for your children but what you have taught them to do for themselves that will make them successful human beings.

—ANN LANDERS

How much fear did I bring to the childbirth experience?

The birth of every new baby is God's vote of confidence in the future of man.

—IMOGENE FEY

If I could go back and change anything about my deliveries, what would it be?

How did I choose the name of each child?

Did I breast-feed? For how long?

What do I think about circumcision?

What was my husband's part in pregnancy and delivery? How was I feeling about him during that time?

What style of discipline did I attempt to use with my children? Would I use the same general approach again?

What is one thing I know I did right in raising my children?

What is one thing I might do differently if I could raise my children again?

If any of my children are adopted, what has been the greatest reward and the greatest challenge of that? How have people close to me experienced adoption?

Do I know anyone who has experienced artificial insemination? How do I feel personally about the idea?

The way to keep children at home is to make home a pleasant atmosphere—and to let the air out of the tires.

—DOROTHY PARKER

The real menace in dealing with a five-year-old is that in no time at all you begin to sound like a five-year-old.

—JEAN KERR

How do I feel about a husband's responsibility in child-rearing? Did my husband participate as I'd hoped?

What aspect of mothering did I find the most rewarding? The most challenging?

What are my feelings about children having pets?

What is one thing I really liked about my own childhood?

What is one thing I did not like that I have tried to make different for my own children?

How do I believe Grandmother experienced childbirth and motherhood?

No matter how old a mother is she watches her middle-aged children for signs of improvement.
—FLORIDA SCOTT-MAXWELL

If you have never been hated by your child, you have never been a parent.
—BETTE DAVIS

Fun

If I were required to spend an entire day doing nothing but "having fun," what would that day look like?

What do I think of amusement parks? Which one that I've been to do I think is the best?

If I had my life to live over again, I would start barefoot earlier in the spring and stay that way later in the fall. I would go to more dances. I would ride more merry-go-rounds. I would pick more daisies.

—Nadine Stair

At what inappropriate place have I ever dissolved into laughter?

He who laughs, lasts.

—Mary Pettibone Poole

If I could vacation anywhere in the world, where would it be?

What game do I remember playing as a child?

What game do I most enjoy playing?

What game do I feel I am absolutely no good at?

What joke do I remember my mother telling me?

What is my all-time favorite movie comedy?

What are some of my most fun childhood memories?

What is one thing I think is fun that you do not? What is one thing you think is fun that I do not?

What non-serious book have I recently read? Do I usually read serious books?

What style of music do I usually listen to? Who are my favorite vocalists?

Family jokes, though rightly cursed by strangers, are the bond that keeps most families alive.

—STELLA BENSON

If you obey all the rules you miss all the fun.

—KATHARINE HEPBURN

What movie title or sitcom title do I feel describes my life?

Do I enjoy giving parties? What kind?

If I could purchase the car of my dreams, what would it be?

Those who do not know how to weep with their whole heart don't know how to laugh either.
—GOLDA MEIR

If I inherited a thousand dollars that had to be spent on something frivolous, what would it be?

You have to sniff out joy, keep your nose to the joy-trail.
—BUFFY SAINTE-MARIE

What is one thing I have collected, just for fun?

What secret, fun indulgence do I look forward to that not everyone knows about?

What did Grandmother do for fun?

Experiences

Name all the different houses I have lived in.

Name all the foreign countries to which I have traveled. If I haven't been out of the country, name the states.

Eat of the fruit of the tree, for it is good and will make us wise, and we shall be as gods.

—Eve

Have I ever met a famous person? What living famous person would I love to meet?

For what has my name ever been in the newspapers? Have I ever been on television? If I have not experienced my allotted fifteen minutes of fame, what do I hope it will be for?

Mistakes are part of the dues one pays for a full life.

—Sophia Loren

Do I keep a diary? When is the last time I wrote in it? Do I let anyone read it? What do I want to have happen to it when I'm gone?

What other historical period would I choose to go back and visit?

What is the greatest physical risk I have taken? What is the greatest physical danger I have ever found myself in?

If they ever create colonies in space, would I be among the first or last to want to live there? Visit there?

Would I ever go mountain climbing? Rappelling? Parasailing? Skydiving? Triathlon running? Skiing? River rafting? Scuba diving? Take pilot lessons? Take belly-dancing lessons? Play the lottery? Check out a racy library book?

If we could sell our experiences for what they cost us, we'd all be millionaires.
—ABIGAIL
VAN BUREN

Courage is the price that Life exacts for granting peace.
—AMELIA EARHART

Have I participated in a protest, or do I write letters to the editor or in other ways try to influence public thought?

What is a funny or embarrassing circumstance in which I found myself?

If I felt strongly impressed to do something, and most of my family and friends were against it, what would I do?

Have I ever won a contest or been awarded a prize?

When was my first airplane ride? Train ride?
Major boat ride?

What is one thing I got in trouble for as a
child or teenager?

What is one thing I thought I could never
accomplish, but I finally did?

If at first you don't succeed, skydiving is not for you.
—ANONYMOUS, ANN LANDERS

How do I feel about speaking, singing, or
performing in public?

Be bold. If you're going to make an error, make a doozy, and don't be afraid to hit the ball.
—BILLIE JEAN KING

What are my fears and phobias?

What is something, physical or mental, I
would love to do but don't believe I will ever
have the motivation to do?

Anonymous was a woman.
—ANONYMOUS

What is something, physical or mental, I
would love to do and believe I will one day
actually do?

What do I remember as a remarkable experience Grandmother had? How did she feel in
general about being adventuresome?

Food

What type of restaurant is my favorite? Least favorite?

What is my favorite forbidden food?

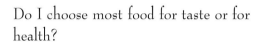

Do I have any rituals around eating?

Is there a meal I generally skip? If I had to skip a meal, which meal would it be?

Life is too short to stuff a mushroom.
—Shirley Conran

Do I choose most food for taste or for health?

A good cook is like a sorceress who dispenses happiness.
—Elsa Schiaparelli

Where do I get most of my protein?

What food did my mother prepare that I liked? What food did my mother prepare that I did not like?

What food has my mother's voice attached to it? "You should . . . you should not . . ."

What food do I crave because it was not in the house in my early years?

What food that I used to hate do I now enjoy? What food did I used to hate and still hate?

What food do I fix for myself if I am totally alone in the house?

What is the grossest thing I've ever eaten?

Cooking is like love. It should be entered into with abandon or not at all.
—HARRIET VAN HORNE

If I were a flavor of ice cream, what would I be?

What did I have for breakfast this morning?

Am I now or have I ever been a vegetarian?

What a nuisance! Why should one have to eat? And what shall we eat this evening?
—COLETTE

If invited to a potluck dinner, what might I choose to bring?

What several spices do I use most often?

Would I rather use butter or margarine? Do I say yes or no to buttering the popcorn in movies?

Do I usually eat whole-wheat bread or white bread?

What do I think about drinking milk? Alcohol? Carrot juice? Herbal teas? Coffee? Black tea? Colas? Other carbonated drinks?

Large, naked, raw carrots are acceptable as food only to those who live in hutches eagerly awaiting Easter.
—FRAN LEBOWITZ

I've been on a constant diet for the last two decades. I've lost a total of 789 pounds. By all accounts, I should be hanging from a charm bracelet.
—ERMA BOMBECK

Life, Death, Spirit

What do I believe about God? How has this belief changed over the course of my life?

What do I believe about fate in general?

Do I believe my life has a destiny or a special calling? Has it been fulfilled?

Do I feel I have had an unusual spiritual experience?

Do I believe in angels?

Do I believe in reincarnation?

Under what star sign was I born? Do I feel that has affected me?

Where do I go or what do I do that makes me feel I have reconnected with my spirit or with God?

What several books have had a major spiritual impact on me?

Every evening I turn worries over to God. He is going to be up all night anyway.

—MARY C. CROWLEY

When I found out God was white, and a man, I lost interest.

—ALICE WALKER

Have I ever had a psychic reading? How did I feel about it?

What recurring dreams have I had, and what do they mean to me?

What do I believe about UFOs, Bigfoot, the Bermuda Triangle, Ouija Boards, Crop Circles, and other unexplained phenomena?

What was my first experience with death?

What do I believe about life after death?

Who are the important people in my life that have passed away? Was I present for any of these deaths? Have any of these deaths changed my life?

Do I have a will? Where is it kept?

Do I have any other plans in place for my own death?

We don't see things as they are, we see them as we are.
—ANAIS NIN

It's better to light a candle than to curse the darkness.
—ELEANOR ROOSEVELT

Do I want my organs to be donated after I die?

Do I believe the world is getting better or getting worse? What do I believe about "the end of the world" or "the shift of the ages"?

If Grandmother is dead, at what age did she pass away? What were or are the major spiritual beliefs or experiences that sustained her?

You don't get to choose how you're going to die. Or when. You can only decide how you're going to live. Now.

—JOAN BAEZ

Death is simply a shedding of the physical body, like the butterfly coming out of a cocoon. . . . It's like putting away your winter coat when spring comes.

—ELISABETH KUBLER-ROSS

Friends

Who is the last friend I spoke to on the telephone?

Is there a friend with whom I had a falling out? Are we still alienated? Do I feel I need to "mend fences" or not?

Do I have a long-term, close, non-romantic male friend?

If something terrible or wonderful happened to me, which friend would I probably call first?

Do I have a friend that I feel takes more than she gives? Is that okay with me or is it a problem?

Two may talk together under the same roof for many years, yet never really meet; and two others at first speech are old friends.

—MARY CATHERWOOD

Treat your friends as you do your pictures, and place them in their best light.

—JENNIE JEROME CHURCHILL

What friend have I helped through a major crisis?

What friend has helped me through a major crisis?

What friend do I wish I could see more often?

Are there people in my life, family or friends, that I consider "thorns in my side?" How do I deal with this?

Is there someone I did not like originally who I now consider a good friend?

What friend makes me laugh the most? With what friend can I have the deepest conversations?

What public figure or past historical figure would I like to be friends with?

What gift from a friend means a great deal to me?

God gives us our relatives; thank God we can choose our friends!
—ETHEL WATTS MUMFORD

Nobody sees a flower—really—it is so small—we haven't time—and to see takes time like to have a friend takes time.
—GEORGIA O'KEEFFE

Do I go to my high school reunions? How do I feel about being there?

Have I ever consciously pulled away from a friendship? Why?

What friend do I feel has had a very positive influence on my life?

A friend is someone who knows the song of your heart, and who sings it to you when memory fails.
—CARMEL DE RENO

Do any of my friends have a nickname for me? Do I have nicknames for some of my friends?

It's the friends you can call up at 4 A.M. that matter.
—MARLENE DIETRICH

Who is my "oldest" good friend? Who is my "newest" good friend?

Do I feel I have the ability to make new friends? Do I feel the need for new friends in my life now?

Did my mother have a wider circle of friends than her mother did? What friends did Grandmother like to talk about?

Relationships with Men

How do I feel about romantic love?

Where, when, and with whom was my first kiss? How did I feel about it?

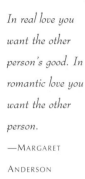

Name all my very important romantic relationships.

In real love you want the other person's good. In romantic love you want the other person.
—Margaret Anderson

Of the men I've dated, who was the biggest disappointment and why?

When did I first meet my current or most significant relationship, and what was our first date?

It doesn't matter what you do in the bedroom as long as you don't do it in the street and frighten the horses.
—Mrs. Patrick Campbell

If I were to describe sex in one word, what would it be?

How did my relationship with my father affect my relationships with men? How is the man in my major relationship like my father? How is he unlike my father?

What did I see in my parents' relationship that I liked? That I didn't like? How has that affected my own relationships?

If I had a poster of a movie star on my wall, who would it be?

What do I feel are the greatest benefits of marriage? The greatest drawbacks?

The only time a woman really succeeds in changing a man is when he's a baby.
—NATALIE WOOD

Would I say that my mother was happy in her marriage?

What marriage that I've seen close up do I admire?

What marriage that I've seen close up do I definitely not admire?

I think it is a grave mistake for young girls to think that it has to be a career versus marriage, equality versus love. Partnership, not dependence, is the real romance in marriage.
—MURIEL FOX

What do I think about divorce in general? Do I know a case in which I believe divorce was a good move? Do I know a case in which I believe divorce was not a good move?

What period of my life was the happiest in terms of a love relationship? What period of my life was the most unhappy?

What do I think about a woman keeping her maiden name when she marries?

What do I think about who pays for what when a couple is dating?

I never hated a man enough to give him diamonds back.

—Zsa Zsa Gabor

If I were attracted to a man, would I make the first move or would I wait for him to do it?

Do I ever play matchmaker for my friends?

How do I feel Grandmother experienced love, sex, and marriage?

The easiest kind of relationship for me is with ten thousand people. The hardest is with one.

—Joan Baez

Life of the Mind

What is a book I recently read and what did I think of it?

If you were to catch me browsing in a bookstore, what section would I probably be in?

What television program do I most look forward to watching? What television program would I *never* watch?

Name six videotapes that I own.

What movie have I seen that I absolutely hated? Movie I loved? Stage play I hated? Stage play I loved?

What magazines do I subscribe to?

Did I have a happy experience in elementary school? What was my transportation there?

How did I feel about my high school experience? Who was my favorite teacher? What were my favorite extracurricular activities? How did I feel about grades?

Did I graduate from college? Which one? What was my major? My minor?

What subject in school did I love? What subject did I really dislike?

Do I feel I am more "book smart" or "street smart"?

Would I describe myself more as a "mental person" or a "physical person"?

How am I continuing my education?

What kind of writing do I enjoy doing?

Am I a stickler when it comes to proper language? What word do I love to use? Do I speak a foreign language?

If you have knowledge, let others light their candles at it.

—MARGARET FULLER

I started that book but something happened, my brother's children, my mother's gall bladder, something happened so I never finished.

—MAUREEN HOWARD

Fuzzy Red Bathrobe

Did I perform in a play or other performance as a child? Did I play a musical instrument? What song or poem do I remember from my childhood?

What opinion have I expressed strongly within the past week? What opinion have I changed over the last few years?

What is one item in the news I have commented on recently? What did I have to say about it? Do I clip news articles?

Do I strongly align myself with a political party?

What do I remember of Grandmother's education? Talents? What cultural or political things did she feel strongly about?

A closed mind is a dying mind.
—EDNA FERBER

He says a learned woman is the greatest of all calamities.
—MARIE EBNER VON ESCHENBACH

Nature

What childhood memories do I have regarding nature? Sights? Smells? Touch? What was my favorite outdoor spot as a child?

What is my favorite outdoor spot near my home today?

Do I notice the cycles of the moon? Which of the star constellations can I readily identify?

In the name of the bee / And of the butterfly / And of the breeze, amen!

—EMILY DICKINSON

How do I feel about the ocean? Do I fear it? Do I enjoy swimming in it? How about scuba diving? Water skiing?

It does not matter a hoot what the mockingbird on the chimney is singing. . . . The real and proper question is: Why is it beautiful?

—ANNIE DILLARD

What is my favorite flower?

Is there a tree that has special memories for me?

What is a memory I have of you and me together out in nature?

Did I or do I like to sunbathe? Do I ordinarily wear sunglasses?

Have I planted a garden? Was it successful?

Have I ever wanted to grow an herb garden?

If I were an animal, what would it be?

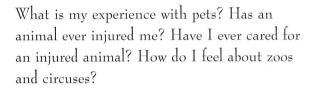

What is my experience with pets? Has an animal ever injured me? Have I ever cared for an injured animal? How do I feel about zoos and circuses?

What is my experience with or feelings about hunting and fishing?

Do I have vivid memories that involve the sun or rain or snow?

Would I rather work outdoors or in?

What is my experience with camping? Do I want to do more of this?

Do I feel prepared to survive in the wilderness if necessary? Have I ever done or wanted to do a survival course or have a vision quest experience?

Perhaps nature is our best assurance of immortality.

—ELEANOR ROOSEVELT

Many times I have looked into the eyes of wild animals. And we have parted friends.

—GRACE SETON-THOMPSON

When outdoors, do I enjoy going barefoot?

What items from nature do I display in my home?

Would I rather spend time at the ocean, in the mountains, or in the desert?

Would I rather sleep in or get up to watch the sunrise?

What was my closest encounter with the forces of nature?

Do I feel I could better handle living where it was unusually hot or unusually cold?

Under what conditions would I ever go skinny-dipping?

What was Grandmother's experience with nature? What did she enjoy? What might have been a challenge?

Whenever someone comes in from outside, with the wind in their clothes and the cold on their cheeks, I feel like burying my head under the blankets to keep from thinking, "When will we be allowed to breathe fresh air again?"
—ANNE FRANK

Sky, be my depth; Wind, be my width and my height.
—LEONORA SPEYER

Work and Dreams

What did I tell people when they asked what I wanted to be when I grew up? Professionally, is that what I became?

What is my dream career, or other path of "following my bliss"? Am I engaged in it now? If not, why not?

If, like Martin Luther King Jr., I have a dream to make the world better, what is it? What have I done in that direction? Is my profession in line with it?

How do I feel you have encouraged me in one of my dreams, professionally or personally?

What is a compromise I have had to make with my work goals on behalf of family? How do I feel about this?

What is one talent or skill that I have not yet developed but have always wanted to?

The future belongs to those who believe in the beauty of their dreams.
—ELEANOR ROOSEVELT

If you think you are too small to be effective, you have never been in bed with a mosquito.
—BETTE REESE

What is one or more dream I have fulfilled that made me very proud of achieving it?

What talent or skill can I develop now only in my dreams?

If I played a musical instrument, what would it be?

Women are expected to do twice as much as men in half the time and for no credit. Fortunately, this isn't difficult.
—CHARLOTTE WHITTON

Trace as best you can my employment history and how I felt about each job.

One can never consent to creep when one feels an impulse to soar.
—HELEN KELLER

How do I feel about my present job? What do I love? Hate?

What job would I hate the very most?

Is my job one that my education prepared me for?

Who is my boss at work and how do I feel about her or him?

Would I rather be self-employed or in a regular work system?

Would I rather work with people or work in solitude?

Have I ever asked for a raise? How do I feel about promoting myself? Do I feel I under-value myself professionally?

Would I rather work at a job I love for low pay or a job I don't like for lots more money?

What are my plans for retirement? How will I then spend my time?

What professional goals did Grandmother have that she either followed or gave up? Professionally or personally, did she "follow her bliss"?

To feel valued, to know, even if only once in a while, that you can do a job well is an absolutely marvelous feeling.
—BARBARA WALTERS

It is easier to live through someone else than to become complete yourself.
—BETTY FRIEDAN

Trials and Tribulations

What possessions have I had stolen?

What natural disasters have I seen or experienced?

What automobile or other accidents have I been in?

What is a trial you or I or both have experienced that I feel brought us closer together?

What major heartbreaking events have forever changed my life?

What is one great sadness in my life out of which something very positive has come?

What loss have I experienced that still causes me pain?

It does not matter what obstacles are in your particular path, but always try to eat happy, walk happy, exercise happy, even cry happy, because today is all we have.
—Katy Pearson
Adams

The actual stress of a life event won't have as much effect on you as the way you perceive that event.
—Mona Lisa
Schulz, M.D.

What recent disappointment have I experienced?

What is one trial that I hope never happens to me?

Do I feel that life's trials are random happenings (good or bad luck) or do I feel there is some meaning behind them?

If I feel there is meaning, do I see a pattern in the challenges that have come into my life?

What trial do I feel you have handled well?

What public figure do I admire for how she or he handled adversity?

What friend or relative do I admire for dealing gracefully with life's trials?

Do I know someone who is trapped in bitterness about disappointments?

Losing our way in life is not only a possibility, it is an experience that is part of the spiritual path. We often don't realize that the way to God is generous and error is part of the journey. As soon as we become conscious that we are lost, we have found our way again.

—Lauren Artress

Self-pity in its early stages is as snug as a feather mattress. Only when it hardens does it become uncomfortable.

—Maya Angelou

What book or movie do I love for its example
of triumph over tragedy?

What is something I have expressed a fear
about?

When is the last time I saw you cry?

*We are healed when
we can grow from
our suffering, when
we can reframe it as
an act of grace that
leads us back to
who we truly are.*

—JOAN BORYSENKO

What is one trial my mother had that I am
grateful I have never had?

What would Grandmother have considered
the trial of her life? How did she deal with
sadness and loss?

*Life is something
that happens to you
while you're making
other plans.*

—MARGARET MILLAR

You and Me

What is one thing I think of as one of your strengths?

What is one thing I remember you doing that still makes me laugh?

Was there a period of time I feel our relationship underwent a major change? When was it?

Do I feel we are moving in the direction of being "friends" as well as "mother and daughter"?

Do I feel a strong need to be either the authority figure or the one who is taken care of?

What is one thing I really like about our relationship?

What is one thing I would like to improve on in our relationship?

What I wanted most for my daughter was that she be able to soar confidently in her own sky, wherever that might be, and if there was space for me as well I would, indeed, have reaped what I had tried to sow.
—HELEN CLAES

It was Mother who fought. Fought! To keep my name in the large type she believed I merited.
—ELSIE JANIS

If I could go back into the past, what is something I might do differently in our relationship?

If you were suddenly gone, what things would I miss the most about you?

What recent thing have you done for me that I really appreciate?

What is one thing you do that annoys me?

What disagreement have you and I had that I feel we settled to both of our satisfaction?

What is something I have seen you do that I have been proud of?

In what way do I feel I am like my mother in my behavior?

In what way do I feel I am unlike my mother in my behavior?

If I had one wish for my children, it would be that each of them would reach for goals that have meaning for them as individuals.

—LILLIAN CARTER

What do girls do who haven't any mothers to help them through their troubles?

—LOUISA MAY ALCOTT

What is a specific thing my mother did that I swore I would never do, but now I do it and I think it's a good thing to do?

What is one comforting smell I associate with my mother?

What is an occasion on which I believe you and I have both been very, very happy?

What is one thing I think you are better at than I am?

If I say prayers for you, what do I pray for?

Are we closer as mother and daughter than Grandmother was to her daughters? Is there something we could learn from her in this?

Let me not forget that I am the daughter of a woman who herself never ceased to flower.

—COLETTE

Yours the voice Sounding ever in my ears.

—MADELINE MASON-MANHEIM

A mother is not a person to lean on but a person to make leaning unnecessary.

—DOROTHY CANFIELD FISHER